KING'S LYNN
MEMORIES OF
THE
1950'S & 1960'S

BY VERA WITT

CONTENTS

DEDICATION.

ACKNOWLEDGEMENTS.

INTRODUCTION.

DEDICATION

I would like to dedicate my book
to my children
and
all my grandchildren

Tuesday Market Place from the Corn Exchange showing
St. Nicholas Chapel steeple.
Courtesy of Dick Goodchild

ACKNOWLEDGEMENTS

I would like to express my sincere gratitude to the people named below, because without their kind generosity in allowing me to use photographs from their photographic collections, this book would not have been possible.

James Tuck
Dick Goodchild
J. Walker
Dr. Andrew Lane, Trues Yard Museum
Malcolm Powell, Lynn News
D. Geary.
A. Barrett.
Mrs R. Wilson
College Of West Anglia
Eastern Daily Press
P. Manning, for the use of the 1957 Kelly's Directory
Front cover photograph Lynn News
Front cover design King's Lynn Press Limited

©Vera Witt 2002
First Printed 2002
Published by ALVER BOOKS
Printed by King's Lynn Press Ltd., Austin Fields, King's Lynn

ISBN O-9513119-2-1

INTRODUCTION

After my last book on King's Lynn, I felt I must recall once again the town in which I was born. I gave this much thought and decided to write about the Lynn of my younger days.

Those of mature years will no doubt remember with affection, as I do, the Lynn of our youth. Those in their forties will only have limited recall, but the youngsters of today will know nothing of how Lynn once looked.

I would therefore like to take you on a journey back in time to the fifties and sixties, before Lynn was partially demolished. Many of the shops changed ownership or tenancy at this time, hence I have chosen the particular year of 1957 to name them.

The arrival of the supermarkets spelt the end for the smaller grocery stores. Some that stand out in my memory include: Ladyman, David Greig, Star Supply, Home & Colonial, International, Liptons, Maypole, Pearks and Melias.

At the time there were three cinemas in the town, Theatre Royal, Pilot and Majestic, the entertainment venues of Lynn. Sadly the Majestic is the only cinema remaining.

King's Lynn was, to coin a phrase, a swinging town. Young men in their Teddy boy outfits, others in suits, sports jackets and neckties. Girls in swirling dresses, mini skirts, bee-hive hairstyles and stilettos.

I have many memories of this era, as I expect do many of you! With the writing of this book I hope I can illustrate King's Lynn as it once looked.

Vera Witt

Tuesday Market Place on market day. Courtesy of Lynn News.

1

TUESDAY MARKET PLACE

In my last book on King's Lynn I began at the Tuesday Market Place. I consider it appropriate to begin here again. Many of you like myself are familiar with the buildings which have not altered a great deal over the years, although some have changed ownership.

In 1957 Barwell & Sons wine merchants were the proprietors of Neale's bar, located next to Lloyds Bank. Neale's bar is now part of Lloyds Bank.

The Dukes Head Hotel has undergone alterations from the fifties to the present day, including further bedrooms, a new ballroom and a car park at the rear. Next to the hotel Ye Olde Maydens Heade, known in the fifties and later as the Maids Head was a popular place.

United Friendly Insurance, Westminster Bank, a Doctors Surgery and The Victory public house are all now incorporated into Ward Gethin Solicitors.

Many buildings have been used by various companies as offices and today still are, for example, Hawkins Solicitors, Leftley Mallett, Unilink, Dental practice, Osteopath Practice, Whiting & Partner and the Driving Theory Test Centre.

The Corn Exchange now refurbished for concerts, was in the fifties used as a dance hall. Dances were held on Saturday nights where people danced to the music of the big bands, Ted Heath, Sid Phillips, Eric Delaney and the Squadronaires to name a few. Many couples met on these occasions and eventually married, including myself.

The Globe Hotel on the corner of King Street and Ferry Lane had a bar at the rear known as the Palm Court where the American servicemen from Sculthorpe were frequent visitors. Many marriages between the Americans and local girls resulted from their meetings there. Some on their return to King's Lynn years later, looked for the building, unfortunately no longer as they remembered it.

The Market Square was on occasions the scene of many a fracas between the local Teddy boys, American servicemen and the R.A.F. servicemen. These usually occurred on Saturday nights when they all gathered for a good time.

The yearly Mart was also something to look forward to with its Waltzers, Ben Hur and the Swing Boats. However the rides today are much more sophisticated.

Barclays Bank and the Woolpack public house were both refurbished in the fifties and Neville Pearson Estate Agents and Jai's Chemist now occupy the premises that was Jones & Dunn Outfitters.

Tuesday Market Place showing Woolpack on corner.
Courtesy of Dick Goodchild

Market House, Tuesday Market Place. Courtesy of Dick Goodchild.

4

Tuesday Market with Corn Exchange, Hill House and Bishops House. Courtesy of Dick Goodchild.

Tuesday Market from Corn Exchange, showing Dukes Head Hotel. Courtesy of Dick Goodchild.

6

Tuesday Market Place showing Barclays Bank and Globe Hotel. Courtesy of Dick Goodchild.

View of Tuesday Market Place showing Victory public house on corner. Courtesy of R. Wilson.

Tuesday Market Place on a busy day, showing Jones & Dunn on corner. Courtesy of Dick Goodchild.

HIGH STREET

High Street with its many shops was in the 1950's and 1960's the centre of King's Lynn. On Tuesday market days it was usually crowded with people and was open to traffic, but nowadays like the rest of town it is pedestrianised. Some of the shops I have to admit I never visited, everybody had his or her own personal choice of store. Some evenings we would walk around the town like many others did, window gazing, looking at the items that caught our eye. The elegant gowns in the more elite shops, the array of jewellery in the windows and the record shop window display for the hits of the day.

FROM THE TUESDAY MARKET PLACE LEFT SIDE

MIDLAND BANK.
EVE gowns (now THE EDINBURGH WOOLLEN MILL).
SKETCHLEYS dry cleaners (now THE IMPERIAL CANCER FUND CHARITY SHOP).
MARKS & SPENCER department store where I purchased my lingerie.
BRIGGS & CO shoe shop (now ORANGE) where I bought children's shoes.
ALLEN& NEALE chemist (now PHONES 4 U).
MODELIA ladies wear (now CANCER CHARITY SHOP) where I bought skirts, jackets and my wedding outfit.
FINLAY & CO tobacconist.
JOHNSON BROS Ltd dyers (now ESSEX SHOE REPAIRS).
GALLYON & SON gunsmiths (now THE BODY SHOP).
RIVETT drapers (now CLINTON CARDS).
A.B. WOODCOCK Ltd confectioners (now ETAM) where we would treat ourselves weekly to cream cakes.
GODDARD Ltd outfitters (now LUNN POLY TRAVEL AGENT and LAURA ASHLEY).
FREEMAN HARDY & WILLIS Ltd shoe shop (now BAY TRADING CO).
EAST ANGLIAN TRUSTEE SAVING BANK (now ALLSPORTS).
QUEENS HEAD public house, publican J. TOZER (now ELECTRONICS BOUTIQUE).

BOOTS CHEMIST where I acquired nail scissors, bath salts by the packet, make up, shaving sticks and perfume.
HIPPS mens outfitters, my husband bought his wedding suit here.
J. H. LADYMAN & CO LTD retail grocers (now LITTLEWOODS).

Overhead there were cables that ran across this shop to a central cashpoint. The assistant put your money into a wooden container, pulled a handle which sent it flying across the shop and then the cashier would return your change in the same manner. When my children were young they were always eager to visit the shop. They watched in childish amazement as the containers travelled overhead. The smell of coffee that came from within filled the air outside. I suspect those of us who can still remember will recall that delicious aroma. Ladyman's also had an excellent gallery restaurant and cafeteria.

However, I cannot close my writing on Ladyman's without mentioning the red teapot that hung outside the shop, now in the King's Lynn Museum.

MAYPOLE DAIRY CO Ltd grocers (also now LITTLEWOODS), where one could watch the assistant expertly pat butter from a large block with wooden patters, shaping it into a pound or half as the customer desired.

BENEFIT LTD shoe shop and STAR SUPPLY grocers
(now VISION EXPRESS).
BARRETT footwear.
LONDON CENTRAL MEAT and FOSTER BROS menswear (both now BOOTS OPTICIANS).

NEW CONDUIT STREET

HILTONS LTD boots & shoes (now SHOE ZONE).
HEPWORTHS LTD tailors (now STATIONERY BOX).
W. H. SMITH & SON newsagents (now LLOYDS BANK).

LE GRICE BROS Ltd. fashion & fabrics (now WILKINSON).

This store was my first place of employment on leaving school, where I worked on a counter with a Miss Wildbur. Our counter contained men's longjohns, flannel shirts, gloves, boxed handkerchiefs, childrens woollen vests, socks and nylons, which were scarce in those days and were allocated with shrewdness by Miss Wildbur. Personally I was only allowed to buy two pairs of "nylons" per month. If they laddered they would be taken to FORUM'S DRYCLEANERS who endeavoured to mend them invisibly.

LENNARDS Ltd shoe shop (now YORKSHIRE BANK).

MURDOCH'S music shop and TURNER bootmaker (both now ABBEY NATIONAL bank).

SMITH & SON dry cleaners (now RUSSEN & TURNER ESTATE AGENTS).

HEATH & HEATHER health food shop (now GOING PLACES).

UNION LANE

JERMYN & SONS Ltd department store (now DEBENHAMS). This usually had a good selection of gents ties, fashion and furniture.

EASTER radio services (now THE CARPHONE WAREHOUSE).

CHESHIRE CHEESE public house (now STARTRITE SHOES).

HARTLEY Ltd drapers (now BENSON FOR BEDS).

HEYS confectioners and LOWN & CAPPS printers (both now FULL MONTY PINE FURNITURE).

T. HAMBLIN opticians (now HARRISON HOLIDAYS).

KETTERING & LEICESTER shoes (now GIBSONS).

A. SMITH jeweller (now HIGH STREET NEWS).

Allen & Neale on corner of Norfolk St. and High St. No longer a chemist. Courtesy of Lynn News.

High St. looking towards New Conduit St. showing Rivetts, Woodcocks and George Goddards.
Courtesy of James Tuck

Earlier view of Freeman, Hardy & Willis.
Courtesy of Dick Goodchild.

An earlier photograph of Queens Head public house, High St.
Courtesy of J. Walker.

High Street, showing demolition of Ladymans. Courtesy of Dick Goodchild.

Ladyman & Co., demolished. Now site of Littlewoods.
Courtesy of James Tuck.

18

High St., looking towards New Conduit St. Courtesy of Dick Goodchild.

High St., looking towards Saturday Market Place, showing Hepworths, W. H. Smith & Son and Le Grice Bros. Courtesy of James Tuck.

High St., showing Le Grices on right. Courtesy of Dick Goodchild.

High St., corner of Union Lane, showing Heath & Heather. Courtesy of Dick Goodchild.

Jermyns, High St. Courtesy of Dick Goodchild.

23

View of High St. from Burtons Outfitters on left. Courtesy of Dick Goodchild.

An early photograph of Ketteringham shoeshop. Courtesy of Dick Goodchild.

HIGH STREET
FROM THE TUESDAY MARKET PLACE RIGHT SIDE

JONES & DUNN outfitters (now JAI CHEMISTS).

WALTON BROS tailors (now EARLY LEARNING CENTRE).

E. SWAIN photographer (now SCOPE).

RANDALL Ltd shoes (now JESSOPS CAMERA SHOP).

TARGETT stationers (now HELP THE AGED).

H. SAMUEL jewellers,

PEATLING & CAWDRON wines & spirits (now McDONALDS).

KIRK shoe shop (now HALIFAX BANK).

Another shop where customers were treated with politeness no matter how many pairs of shoes they tried on, I bought my wedding shoes here.

WOOLWORTH STORES (now SUPER DRUG & DIXONS).

A very versatile store where one could buy almost anything from reels of cotton, pots & pans, tins of paint, clothes, sweets, spacious enough to manoeuvre a pram around.

EASIEPHIT shoe shop.

Many pairs of shoes bought here, having a larger size made it difficult to get shoes that were fashionable, I did manage however to buy a pair of stilettos known as winkle pickers, trendy but not so clever if the heel caught in the cracks between the pavement slabs.

Easiephit & Rivett now

RIVETT wool shop. (WATERSTONES BOOKS).

DOLCIS shoes (now TRAVEL CHOICE).

NORFOLK NEWS CO Ltd EASTERN DAILY PRESS.

PURDY baker (now DOLLAND & AITCHISON).

S. BURLINGHAM jewellers (now BIRTHDAY CARD SHOP).

CURRY Ltd cycles, radio, television (now NEXT).

HEAD dress shop (now SIZE UP).

BROWN BROS & TAYLOR furniture (now CLARKS SHOES).

When married some of our furniture was bought here.

ROSE leathergoods (now RIVER ISLAND LADIES & GENTS WEAR).

WESTON Ltd dress shop.

Always had a good selection of skirts and dresses, I bought a black & white dress, old fashioned by today's standards. In those days young ladies seldom wore trousers.

BELFAST LINEN WAREHOUSE CO Ltd.

Many items were bought over the years, beds, curtains, towels, bed linen, tea cloths, cushions & covers.   Weston & Belfast
(now H.M.V Store).

SPEED jeweller (now DOROTHY PERKINS).

My wedding ring was purchased here.

SCOTCH WOOL SHOPS (now THORNTONS).

I often knitted many items, I bought my wool here.

SCOTT & SON hardware, dustpans, brushes, rope, fibre matting, galvanised dustbins, china-ware, furniture, toys and garden implements, a versatile store. The building was demolished to make way for new development. The site now occupied by (MOTHERCARE, BAKERS OVEN, BOOTS CHEMIST).

BURTONS TAILORS mens outfitters,

FLETCHER butchers (now TINY COMPUTERS).

DAVID GREIG Ltd provisions (now ZENITH WINDOWS).

This shop held a special appeal for shoppers, customers could buy from a vast range of cheeses cut from large slabs by the counter staff, with a wire cutter that sliced neatly through to the pound in weight. Biscuits could be bought by the pound e.g. Custard Creams, Shortbread, Malted Milk and Rich Tea. Ham expertly cut from the bone, Mr E.H. BOXALL the manager would teach the assistants this skill, David Greig was also known for their excellent bacon.

FELL & SON cycles (now THOMAS COOK TRAVEL AGENT).

INTERNATIONAL STORE grocer (now ALLIANCE & LEICESTER BANK).

BAKER LANE

BROUGHTON fruiterers (now BRADFORD & BINGLEY BANK).

J. HAMSON menswear (now MOTOR WORLD).

J. HAMSON jeweller (now ABBOTTS ESTATE AGENTS).

HOME & COLONIAL grocers (now WOOLWICH BANK).

WINTON SMITH meats (now HAIR SHARE).
VOGUE ladieswear.   Vogue and John Collier
JOHN COLLIER outfitters,   (now HOGSHEAD public house).
LIPTON provisions (now SAVE THE CHILDREN SHOP).
PALMER & HARVEY tobacconist (now SHOEMANIA SHOES).
ALEXANDRE mens tailors.   Alexandre and Wigram & Ware
WIGRAM & WARE opticians.   (now ARTERTONS FURNITURE).
RICHARD SHOPS ladies wear (now J.J.B. SPORTS).
EBBLING fancy goods (now CLEANBRIGHT DRY CLEANERS).
BROWNS FURNITURE (now SUE RYDER SHOP).
BARNARDS florist (now OXFAM).
SOLESTA coats & gowns.   Solesta and London Central Meat
LONDON CENTRAL MEAT CO.   (now LETS POOL).
WENNS HOTEL public house.

Demolition of Scott & Son. Courtesy of J. Walker.

Earlier view of Waltons in High St. Courtesy of Dick Goodchild.

Scott & Son. Demolished, now Boots Chemist. Courtesy of James Tuck.

Earlier view of Scott & Son, High St. Courtesy of Dick Goodchild.

Barrett's shop, later to become David Greig's. Courtesy of A. Barrett.

High St., David Greig on right. Courtesy of Dick Goodchild.

33

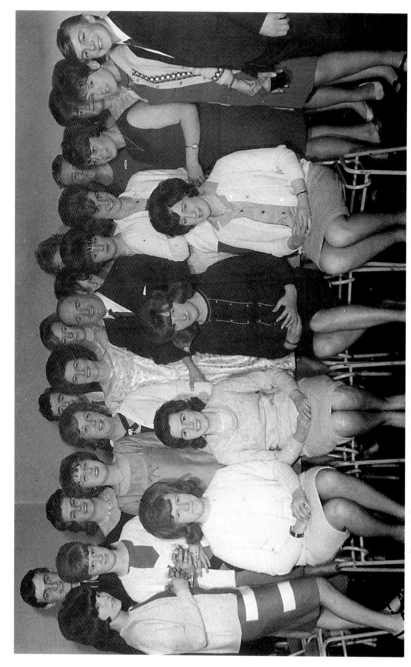

David Greig staff. Mr. E. H. Boxall, manager in centre. Courtesy of Lynn News.

High St. John Collier on right. Courtesy of Dick Goodchild.

NEW CONDUIT STREET

New Conduit Street today looks nothing like it did in the 1950/60's. Services were held at the congregational church and next to this was a small alleyway where the Quaker's meeting house was situated. Captain George Vancouver, one of King's Lynn's seafaring sons was born in New Conduit Street. A statue of him now stands on the Purfleet Quay.

LEFT SIDE

FOSTER BROS mens outfitters.
FRAMES TOURS travel agent (now YANKS).
CLIFFORD LEE couturier (now GOSSIP).
WATER TRANSPORT.
DREDGING & CONSTRUCTION (now NATIONWIDE BANK).
NETHERLANDS VICE-CONSULATE.
EIGHT PRIVATE HOUSES.
NO 11 became KENNETH BUSH SOLICITORS in 1960.
EMPLOYMENT EXCHANGE.
HORNER'S music shop.
CONGREGATIONAL CHURCH.
BELOE & STAVELY solicitors.
Two private houses (became the BRITISH RED CROSS in 1960).
ROYAL LONDON MUTUAL INSURANCE SOCIETY Ltd.
This side of New Conduit Street from number 11 to Baxters Plain was demolished for redevelopment.

RIGHT SIDE

VANCOUVER RESTAURANT, built during the war for servicemen as a canteen, later as a girl's high school dinner hall.
REGAL CAFÉ.
GIFFORD PAGE, antiques dealer.
ESSEX & SUFFOLK INSURERS. This building was used earlier as CUSTANCE & SON TAILORS.
All of these buildings also demolished.

New Conduit St. View from High St. Courtesy of James Tuck.

New Conduit St. View from Baxters Plain. Courtesy of James Tuck.

An earlier photograph of New Conduit St. Courtesy of Dick Goodchild.

39

View of New Conduit St., now site of Argos store. Courtesy of James Tuck.

Vancouvers House, New Conduit St. in state of disrepair. Courtesy of James Tuck.

Vancouvers House, New Conduit St. Courtesy of Dick Goodchild.

Another view of Vancouvers House. Courtesy of Dick Goodchild.

BAXTERS PLAIN

GENERAL POST OFFICE.
W. MILTON butcher (now ANTONIO'S WINE BAR).

SOUTH CLOUGH LANE

EVE RAYNER hairdresser.
MILES chemist.
HOARDING.
Would show from the posters what film was on at the Pilot Cinema
and other advertisements.

SEDGEFORD LANE

BANNISTER tobacconist.
JOAN BILLING hairdresser.

PARADISE PARADE

PET STORES.
JEEP RESTAURANT also frequented by American servicemen.
COLLISON Corn Merchant.
CROME & AKERS Ltd printers.
Where my wedding invitations were printed.
BACON motorcycle agent.
SCOTT wholesale newsagent.
All these buildings demolished (now site of WESTGATE STORE &
SERVICE AREA FOR PREMISES IN ST. DOMINIC SQUARE).

CATTLE MARKET

The entrance to KING'S LYNN MUSEUM was in this street, now
entry is via the Bus Station.

Demolition of most of Baxters Plain. Courtesy of J. Walker.

Miles Chemist, Baxters Plain. Courtesy of J. Walker.

Paradise Parade, now site of Westgate Store and Precinct. Courtesy of James Tuck.

47

TOWER STREET

EDWARDS the florist on the left side would always have fresh blooms of many varieties, this shop is where I would sometimes buy bouquets, and on a sadder occasion a funeral wreath. Drydens the jewellers is where my engagement ring and other items of jewellery came from.

Later when I was married, I was passing ZOO ANIMAL, a puppy looking so forlorn and alone sat huddled in the window, feeling sorry for it I went into the shop and bought him, Sandy was with us for sixteen years.

The Majestic was my place of employment after leaving LE GRICE BROS, I spent many happy hours working here. I started there in July 1952, the film showing at the time was Where the River Bends with James Stewart. This was a time when the cinema was at its peak. The main feature normally started at one thirty pm and was continuous, by the late afternoon long queues had formed reaching as far as New Conduit St, many people did not get to see the film. A popular film at that time was Quo-Vadis. Saturday evening dances were held in the ballroom, now converted into the smaller cinemas. On another occasion the film Calamity Jane with Doris Day was due to be shown, I was chosen if somewhat unwillingly to be dressed in an outfit and walk in the Tuesday Market Place distributing leaflets advertising the film.

As you can see from the photograph, Doris Day I certainly was not. On my day off my boyfriend and I would go to the Pilot Cinema. I left the Majestic and became a GPO telephonist until I married. The Roller Skating Rink was another popular place for youngsters, originally the Wesleyan Chapel until converted. Sometimes we would stop for fish and chips at the Sandringham, they seemed to taste better out of the paper than on a plate, how many of you have done the same I wonder?.

Wheelers on the corner would have the current hit records in their window, our choice however was more in the Frank Sinatra and Ella Fitzgerald mode.

TOWER STREET
FROM BAXTERS PLAIN TO ST JAMES ST LEFT SIDE

EDWARD's florist

DRYDENS jeweller

Edwards and Drydens
(now SCHNELL IMBISS).

SOUTH CLOUGH LANE

P. LOADES (now LADBROKES BOOKMAKER).

J & J DAWSON book & toy shop (now MARTINS BOOKS).

STONE tobacconist,

G. CHARITY baker,

STAINES fruiterer,

Stone, Charity and Staines,
(are all now PASTIMES).

H. BARNABY fishmonger,

BAMBRIDGE fruiterers,

GOODSON fishmonger,

Barnaby, Bambridge and Goodson,
(are all now HARRODS).

DOWNEYS restaurant,

BARNABY& McLEAN wallpaper (also DOWNEYS).

BUSH fish caterer (now SANDRINGHAM RESTAURANT).

WHINCOP HOUSE.

MEDWELL baby linen (now SEAMANS jeweller).

METHODIST CHURCH SCHOOL HALL (now REGENT WAY).

WATTS & ROWE printer (now ROYAL BRITISH LEGION).

RIGHT SIDE

MAJESTIC CINEMA.

GOLDEN BALL public house (now SCAMPS HAIRDRESSER).

BAYES music shop (now BLANCHFORD & MILLS &
SINGER SEWING MACHINE SHOP).

PINK GRILL café (now DEZYNADOG).

Miss A. HILL tobacconist (now MARRS).

G.E. RUHMS hairdresser (now BIJOU).

UNION LANE

VERRY & SON sport outfitters (now DAVIDS COOKWARE).

WATSON picture framers (now PAULINES PANTRY).

BATTERBEE pork butchers (now CHINA & GLASSWARE).

W. LANCASTER pork butcher (now ANNE KENNEDY).

I.G.R. ISLES wool shop (now TREASURE HOUSE GIFTS).
ZOO ANIMAL pet shop (now NORBURY FINE FOODS).
MODEL SHOP (now PINE & THINGS).
J. BROOKER MOTOR CYCLE AGENT & TOWER ROLLING
SKATING RINK (now COOPER ELMS, ECONOMY FLOORING &
REGENTS WAY).
F. WITTRED tobacconist (now DAVID'S SUGARCRAFT).
C. CRESEY bootmaker (now TACKLE BOX).
WHEELERS radio & television dealers (now HOCUS POCUS).

Dressed as Calamity Jane, April 1954. author.

The Majestic Cinema, Tower St. Courtesy of J. Walker.

Tower Street viewed from St. James St, on the left W. H. King second hand cars. Formerly the Wesleyan Chapel, then the Roller Skating Rink. Courtesy of James Tuck.

Sandringham Restaurant, Tower Street. Courtesy of J. Walker.

Wesleyan Chapel, Tower Street, later the roller skating rink. Courtesy of J. Walker.

WHITE HART public house.
COUNTY ELECTRICAL SERVICES.
KING'S LYNN Y.M.C.A (now R.A.O.B. SOCIAL CLUB).
H.W. PEAK furnishers, now empty.
ST. JAMES HOUSE (St. James Club) KING'S LYNN
CONSERVATIVE CLUB, DEMOLISHED (Site is now occupied by
DAVIS SIMPSON & DAVIS PRINTERS and LYNNLEC).
The gateway of St James house now roadway to Car Park.
E. DENNIS pork butchers.   (Dennis and Hall now
F. HALL milliner.   PRONTAPRINT).
MURDINS TYPEWRITERS CO Ltd (now KING'S LYNN BED &
SOFABED CENTRE).
E. LOVEDAY tobacconist (now BOLDERO'S HAIR CO's).
BRIDGE newsagent,
D. WARD green grocer (now THE OLD CURIOSITY SHOP).
SENIORS hairdressers (now BOULTONS & SEYMOUR).
BEARS corn merchants (now KEELING'S HAIR STUDIO).
WHEELERS OF TOWER ST CORNER, (now HOCUS-POCUS).
THE RUMMER public house (now FENTON INSURANCE).
BUILDING MATERIAL (now THAI ORCHARD RESTAURANT).
EMLEN CAFÉ, now THE INDIA GATE RESTAURANT.
S. GOODING hairdresser (now ELYSIAN HAIR & BEAUTY).
N. DOBSON confectioner (now PAULA'S CHILDREN).
STUDIO JOHN NORMAN (now BRIDGET'S FLOWERS).
The photograph of myself as Calamity Jane taken here.
THE LANTERN CAFÉ (now CADENZA CAFÉ).
W. CROME decorator.   Crome, Bucks and Tower Café (now
BUCKS newsagent.   THORNALLEY FUNERAL
TOWER CAFÉ.   SERVICES)

Bears Corn, Flour & Seed shop, St. James St. Courtesy of J. Walker.

Part of St. James Street. Courtesy of R. Wilson.

SATURDAY MARKET PLACE

TRINITY GUILDHALL.
MEDINA GALLERY antique dealers.
J. BETTS shopkeeper (now incorporated into WENNS).
WENNS HOTEL public house.
ST. MARGARETS CHURCH.
MAUDES general outfitters (now GERRY'S PIZZA).
E. PRIOR butcher.
DUKE OF FIFE public house (now LYNN POTTERY).
G. BULLEN confectioner (now PICTURE GALLERY WORKSHOP).
CRISP chemist.
C. BARRETT launderers.
H.W. PEAK furnisher (now PIZZA EXPRESS).

ST JAMES STREET RIGHT SIDE

W. REES watchmaker.
PRATT & COLDHAM hairdressers (now MR SNIPPERS GENTS HAIRDRESSERS).
H.W. PEAK furnishers (now SIZZERS HAIR DESIGN).
Misses WESTWOOD confectioners (now KEVIN PLAYER HAIRDRESSER).
G. BOWERS butcher (now KAA DEE GIFT SHOP).
BENSLEYS cycle & radio shop (now THE RECORD SHOP & NEW DIMENSIONS LADIES WEAR).
THREE PIGEONS public house (now HOWARDS LADIES WEAR).
EASTERN CLEANERS Ltd (now ANGLIA SURVEYORS & GRANVILLE ASSOCIATES).
W.H. JOHNSON motor engineers (now WEST ANGLIA IFAS).
EASTERN GAS BOARD (now ST JAMES ST. LAUNDERETTE).
R. TAYLOR fruiterer (now DRAGON CAPITAL TAKE AWAY).
W.H. JOHNSON office (now HOMEMAKERS).
MADAME AUDREY hairdresser.
BENNELL bakers.
A. SAWER butcher.
W.H. JOHNSON motor engineers (now DEZYNAPET PETS PARADISE & PURE).
THEATRE ROYAL CINEMA (now GALA BINGO).

GREYFRIARS TOWER GARDENS. A delightful park, where on a sunny evening one could sit in peace and quietness. Unaware that prior to 1538 private burials had taken place in Greyfriars, and the park that we know today was opened in 1911. The memorial to the war dead was built after the First World War.

St. Margarets Church. Courtesy of D. Geary.

Greyfriars Park. Courtesy of J. Walker.

A sunny day in Greyfriars Park. Courtesy of the Lynn News.

BROAD STREET

Broad Street was on my route to work, or to visit my Aunt who with her husband ran REEDS Newsagents.

Passing the old cinemas, no longer in use as such, but in their heyday showed silent movies where the pianist would play music suited to the action of the film, a far cry from todays modern films.

Mrs Wilsons secondhand shop where one could buy a book in good condition. She also sold second hand comics popular with the children, if they had missed getting a copy they could catch up with the exploits of the characters in the BEANO and the DANDY, she usually had some available.

THE GROSVENOR CAFÉ.

Where one could buy the new espresso coffee, hear the latest pop records on the Jukebox. In the early fifties the top records were for example, Doris Day's (Secret Love), Frankie Laine's (Jezabel), Guy Mitchell's (She Wore Red Feathers), Jo Stafford's (Shrimp Boats). One song that always seemed to be playing on the jukebox as you passed was Kay Starr's (Wheel of Fortune). Later when rock and roll became popular it was Bill Haley's (Rock Around The Clock).

The Grosvenor was the place to be seen in, used by the locals and also by the American Servicemen, it certainly did swing. The Whisky-A-Go-Go, later became the popular place with the youngsters.

BROAD STREET
FROM BAXTERS PLAIN RIGHT SIDE

EASTMANS butchers.   Both these buildings became
J. GRIFFIN greengrocer.   (WHISKY-A-GO-GO).
MISS CHILVERS babies linen shop.
J. HILLARD fried fish shop.
F. DREW boot repairs.
W&T AVERY scale makers.
CUSTANCE & SON tailors.
NORWICH RELAY radio relay operators.
J. CHILVERS boot repairer, later Spare Moments wool shop.
KING'S LYNN PRESS printers.
BROAD STREET DINING ROOMS café.
REED newsagents.

CATTLE MARKET

THE ELECTRIC THEATRE long out of use as a theatre but later
used by TAYLOR MOTOR ENGINEERS.
M. FINKELBLECH jeweller.
RYDER & CROSSKILL confectioners.
L.E. TAYLOR MOTOR ENGINEERS frontage.
Three private houses.
CATLEUGHS' OF LYNN outfitters.

BROAD STREET FROM BAXTERS PLAIN LEFT SIDE

MAISON ANDREE hairdressers.
J.W. SLATER ironmongers.
SEXTON BROS wholesale fruit merchants.
BRITANNIC ASSURANCE.
PRACTICAL CLOTHING.
Three Private houses.
KING'S LYNN ROYAL BRITISH LEGION (CLUB).
EMPIRE THEATRE long out of use.
WILSON second hand dealer.
HEDGE & CO fishing tackle dealers.

J. BARNABY & SON fish merchants.
CROME & SONS heating engineers.
CATTLE MARKET TAVERN public house.

BAPTIST YARD

P. HANWELL tailor.
MRS RYE fruiterer.

BATHS YARD

FURBANK funeral director.
CLIFTON HOUSE Ltd, furniture.

THE GROSVENOR CAFÉ part of the Grosvenor Hotel.
ALL THE BUILDINGS IN BROAD STREET DEMOLISHED,
EXCEPT FOR CATLEUGHS.

Whisky-A-Go-Go, just before demolition. Courtesy of J. Walker.

The Empire Theatre Cinema, Broad Street.
Courtesy of Trues Yard.

65

Broad Street, showing the Old Empire Theatre. Courtesy of James Tuck.

King's Lynn Press in Broad Street, opposite Empire Theatre. Courtesy of J. E. Hoare.

Broad Street, showing part of the cattle market on the right. Courtesy of James Tuck.

Broad Street, view from Norfolk Street, Old Electric Theatre on left. Courtesy of James Tuck.

Broad Street, view from Norfolk Street, showing Catleughs of Lynn. Courtesy of James Tuck.

NORFOLK STREET

This street was with High Street always bustling with shoppers, although when I was compiling my book I noticed that there seemed to be more shops compared with High Street, this was probably due to the fact that the shops were smaller, except for the odd one or two. If I wanted to shop in town after collecting the children from Highgate School, I would go via Littleport street and return home through Albert Street /Austin Street, calling at Shaws nursery shop for fresh eggs, before going into Chapel Lane and Pilot Street.

The Cattle Market was held on Tuesdays, entrance could be gained via Paradise Lane next to Goodchild photographers, cattle sheep and pigs were kept in pens, the poultry and rabbits in a large shed. I sometimes took the children to see the animals when on their school holidays, they enjoyed seeing them although I personally found the smell unpleasant. The Cattle Market is now the site of The Bus Station, Sainsbury Supermarket and St. Dominics Square.

The Fent Shop, Norfolk Street, previously Wilsons fashions.
Courtesy of J. Walker.

NORFOLK STREET
FROM HIGH ST. LEFT SIDE

MARKS & SPENCER SIDE ENTRANCE.
MANN EGERTON & CO LTD motor engineer (incorporated
into Marks & Spencer.).
MILLETT clothiers (now THE LINK).
TAYLOR seed & bulb merchant (now B' WISE).
DONALDSON fish merchant (now NEW LOOK).
BARRONS men outfitters.   Barrons and Forum
FORUM dry cleaners.   (now SHARPS BEDROOMS).
WINTON SMITH cooked meat.   Winton Smith and Hall
C. HALL furnishers.   (now OTTAKARS BOOK SHOP).
LONDON CENTRAL MEAT CO (now THE FILLING STATION
TAKE AWAY).
HIRST jeweller (now HARWAYES).

TURNER ladies & gents hairdresser (now RAGE FOOTWEAR).
A quaint shop with a character all of its own, where the window
was always full to brimming with hair commodities, slides, combs,
brushes, ribbons and wigs.

CHAIN LIBRARY (now SNAPPY SNAPS).
FLOWER POT public house.
WILSON ladies wear later the FENT SHOP.

EMMERSON & LANGFORD ironmongers. This shop was filled
with an assortment of different hardware products, nails, screws,
garden spades, garden forks, rakes and hoes.

LANGFORD & FIDMENT tobacconist.
The Flower Pot, Wilson, Emmerson & Langford and Langford &
Fidment were all demolished. (now Q.D. STORES).
CULEY corn merchant (now NORFOLK TELECOM).
CLARKE butchers (now NORFOLK TEAROOM).
BAXTERS fruiterer (now SCOTT & SON).

STRATFORD Ltd
Purchased H.J. socks, boot socks for fishermen, flannel shirts and
wool gloves. A good selection of merchandise.

MELIA grocer.
EBBLING fancy goods (now GOBLIN'S PANTRY).
This shop is where I would usually buy my knitting needles, buttons, and pins.
PEARK'S DAIRIES LTD provisions.
GAZLEY outfitters (now Ali's KEBAB HOUSE).
REYNOLDS baker (now NATURAL INTERIOR CURTAINS).
COOLSON ELECTRICS (now ABBEY BLINDS).
BRAY newsagents (now WALKERS NEWS).
WOODCOCK bakers (now D.I.Y. CENTRE).
HAYES chemist (now ANGLIAN WINDOWS).
STEWARD BROWN drapers (now PICTURE FRAME SHOP).
I bought most of the childrens clothing here when they were small.
WHITELEY & CREASY LTD caravans, later ELMO STORE.
The site is (now YOUNGSTERS TOY WORLD).
The next site was empty in 1957, but by 1960 the EAGLE HOTEL and LIMBERTS FISH & CHIP SHOP had been rebuilt, both these buildings were bombed in 1942 with considerable loss of life.
The EAGLE (now THE ORANGE HOUSE).
LIMBERTS (now TOFFS).
VAN PELT pork butchers.
TOWLER hairdresser (now BOBBLYNS).
KING'S LYNN CO/OP butchers (now FLAMES).
THOMAS pork butcher (now WOLFY'S VIDEO).
This is where I would buy pork pies, and sausages.

CALIFORNIA YARD

NORWICH ARMS public house (now HARVEST FIELDS BOOKS).
SCUPHAM pork butchers (now RIDOUTS BAKERS).
BARRETT & CO launderers (now COLLECTORS SHOP).
BARGATE china dealer (now DEWHURST TROPHY CENTRE).

M. BARNES leather merchants (now COUNTRY KITCHENS).
A shop I occasionally visited to buy shoe polish, shoe laces, leather belts also segs that you could put onto the heels of shoes so they would wear longer. When the shop was about to close I went in, and to my amazement found two spinning tops, similar to the ones I used to play with as a child. I still have them.

HOWARD clothier (now JUNK & DISORDERLY).
VALENTINE wine & spirit merchant (now NORFOLK ST
FISH BAR).
SPAXMAN dairyman (now D.K. APPLIANCES).
G. TURNER post office (now SUZYS HAIR DESIGN).
MODERN BOOT REPAIR CO (now HOT POT TAKEAWAY).
EAST ropemaker.   East, Dinky, Andrews and Railway
DINKY hairdresser.   Passage. All demolished
ANDREWS chemist.   (now JOHN KENNEDY ROAD).
RAILWAY PASSAGE.
KING'S LYNN CO-OPERATIVE SOCIETY demolished.
(now site of LIDL STORE).
ATTOS YARD, where my Grandmother was born.
TWO private houses.
BENNETT agricultural engineers.   both now
BRADFIELD & IBBERSON warehouse.   (M.& J CERAMICS).
DAWBER TOWNSLEY & CO building contractors (now
SUPER SEAL CONSERVATORIES).
LIMBERTS fish & chip shop (now HAIR TIPS).
Private house (now FLINTS RESTAURANT).
SCAIFES house furnisher (now JOHN SAVAGE MUSIC).

Norfolk Street from High Street. Courtesy of Dick Goodchild.

75

The Flower Pot public house, Norfolk Street.
Courtesy of J. Walker.

The Eagle Hotel, Norfolk Street. Courtesy of Dick Goodchild.

Maurice Barnes Leathergoods, Norfolk Street.
Courtesy of J. Walker.

NORFOLK STREET
RIGHT SIDE FROM HIGH STREET

LONDON KIOSKS.

THOMPSON fruiterer (now THE WORKS).

DEWHURST butcher (now YOUNGS CAMERAS).

LOWES restaurant.

W. ELY & SON bakers (now EARNEST JONES).

BARNETT-HUTTON costumiers (now FRANCIS WAIN).

EASTERN ELECTRICITY SHOWROOM (now SUPASNAPS).

PLOWRIGHT PRATT & HARBAGE ironmonger (now W.H. SMITH
and JARROLDS).

SINGER SEWING MACHINE CO Ltd (now SAVERS).

R. MONEY leathergoods (now ANDY'S RECORDS).

A good place to purchase a handbag or purse.

FIDDAMANS HOTEL public house (now OFFICERS CLUB).

NICHOLLS & CAMPBELL wine & spirit merchants
(now COMPUTER PLUS).

THE GROSVENOR HOTEL site (now LABELS).

BROAD STREET

CATLEUGHS OF LYNN LTD outfitters (now HOLLAND &
BARRETT and SHOWBOAT HOLDINGS).

W. LOCK & SON contractors (now MOSS & LEAKEY).

C. LOCK butcher (now TOP FROCK & HATS GALORE).

BRIGHTER HOME STORES wallpaper merchants
(now THE PARTY SHOP).

BIRD-IN-HAND public house   Bird-in-Hand and Davy Bros.
DAVY BROS draper   (now PALMERS HOMESTORE).

Little Davies as it was known, sold whale bones for corsets,
full length Pinafores, childrens bonnets, liberty bodices, (worn
during the war instead of vests). Hair ribbons, button hooks for
shoes. Many items from a long forgotten era, although some of
their stock was modern.

CROWN WALLPAPER STORE (now BALMFORTH PROPERTY
RENTALS).

KIRKLANDS Ltd tailors (now DOCTOR THIRSTY'S,
LYNN MUSIC, LYNN GOLD).

A. TWITE greengrocer (now ELECTRIC BEACH SUNBEDS &
THE GREEN OLIVE TREE).
CULEY fruiterer (now R.S.P.C.A. CHARITY SHOP).
MILLER fish & chips (now THE EGG SHOP).
CUTLERS cutler (now BRITISH RED CROSS CHARITY SHOP).
WATSON tobacconist (now GOLD CRAFT).
E. WHARTON boot repairs (now STEWARD BROWN).
P.M. GOODCHILD & SON photographers (now WOODEN TOPS).
Where my children had their first photographs taken at the age
of six months.

PARADISE LANE

HARRISON & WILSON saddlers (now DECK OF CARDS).
W.H. SMITH newsagents (now ROWLINSON & SON).
PANKS printers.
DORANNE infants & childrens wear (now KING 'S LYNN
GLASS & TRIMMING).
T. EDMUNDS hardware (now METRIC CARPETS).
S. RICHES fishmonger (now THE TOWN GOLDSMITH).
G. RICHES tool merchant (now M. CHILVERS).
No. 39 Site empty, but earlier occupied by the SUN HOTEL.
Later New Plowrights Hardware (now CHICAGO ROCK CAFÉ).
T. SADLER toy shop (now ZIA'S CHILLI MASTERS).
SOLESTA costumier (now THE PRIVATE SHOP).
KERSHAW confectioners.
F. MASTERS shoe shop (now GIZMO'S GIFT SHOP).
C. TOWNSEND corn merchant, now boarded up.

RAILWAY ROAD

C. BARBER butcher (now FLOWER CORNER).
ADA WATERS confectioner (now LYNN'S BEST KEBAB HOUSE).
Private house (now STREAMLINE CABS).
Misses EAST confectioners (now CK PET GROOMING).
C. BACK newsagent (now GENESIS HAIRDRESSER).
Two private houses.
H. MORLEY butcher   both these shops are now
C. ASH tobacconist   private houses.

BOOTH radio & television engineers (now HAIR SHAPES).
STEBBING greengrocer (now GRANTS RESTAURANT).
Private house.
W. MASON butcher later COGGLES FUNERAL DIRECTORS.
(now unoccupied)

KIRBY STREET

Three private houses.
TRIXIES wool shop.
R.A.P RENTED RADIO Ltd (now NORFOLK ST. TRADING).
MRS CLEMENTS shopkeeper   Both these shops are now
P. CHAPMAN greengrocer   (MAGPIE SECURITY
                                                          SERVICES).

BLACKFRIARS   ROAD

Earlier view of Plowright & Pratts, Norfolk Street. Courtesy of Dick Goodchild.

The Grosvenor, Norfolk Street.
Courtesy of Dick Goodchild.

Norfolk Street looking towards High Street. Courtesy of James Tuck.

View of Norfolk Street, showing Davy Bros. & the Bird in the Hand public house. Courtesy of James Tuck.

Norfolk Street, looking towards Broad Street, showing Kirklands. Courtesy of James Tuck.

The Cattle Market. Courtesy of Lynn News.

LITTLEPORT STREET
AT JUNCTION OF AUSTIN STREET

CHILVERS cycles & pram shop on corner. This is where I bought
my first pram a traditional style, the second was a pushchair type.
I also purchased my cycle here.
Site now a Shrubbery.

SAUNDERS YARD

DOCKERILL building contractor, years earlier this building
was the fever hospital. (now FLATS).
BLAND boarding house.
Two private houses. (now all KING'S YARD).
DONOVANS YARD,
Private house.
SANDRINGHAM public house.
LAYTONS dry cleaners.
POWELL decorator
PECKOVER general store, later Alec Ford Pet Shop
J. HORGAN Doctor, (now EASTGATE HOUSE
RESIDENTIAL HOME).

KETTLEWELL LANE

LITTLEPORT   STREET
AT JUNCTION OF BLACKFRIARS ROAD

DUKE OF EDINBURGH public house.
Three Private houses
Now site of Flats.
LYNN SERVICE STATION.

LITTLEPORT TERRACE

HOB-IN-THE-WELL public house.
Site of the old East Gate.

Duke of Edinburgh, public house, Littleport Street. Courtesy of J. Walker.

CHAPEL STREET
LEFT SIDE FROM NORFOLK STREET

Private house.
TOWLER & FRENCH hairdressers (now D. AUKER jeweller).
LAIDLOW furniture.
TURNER shopkeeper.

SURREY STREET

DENNIS pork butchers (now T. CLAYTON jeweller).
HAYES & SON plumbers.
KING'S LYNN COLD STORAGE   (now DUKES HEAD HOTEL.
NICHOLLS bookseller.   Car park).

MARKET LANE

J. WHYMARK verger of St Nicholas Chapel (now LATTICE
HOUSE Public house, built about 1470).
EASTERN COUNTY UTILITIES.
Private house.
WHEATLEY grocer.
Misses E & D THOMPSON babywear.
Two private houses.

CHAPEL STREET RIGHT SIDE

EMERSON & LANGFORD ironmonger.
RICHES tool dealer   (all three now site of Q.D. Stores).
WOOLLARD butcher.
During the war I spent a long time at Woollards in a queue with
my mother, in the hope of getting some meat, (not always lucky).
On one occasion some whale meat was available, boiled it was a
dark meat and very tough, we never tried anymore.
EVERITT rag & bone merchants yard.
Four Private houses. Demolished, new housing on site.
BLACK HORSE public house, publican Bush.
WESTGATE HOUSE.

KING'S LYNN LABOUR CLUB, (ST AUGUSTINES)
Demolished.
(BOROUGH COUNCIL OFFICES now occupy site).

AUSTIN STREET

Private house (now LABOUR PARTY HEADQUARTERS).
Private house, now offices.

The Lattice House before refurbishment.
Courtesy of Dick Goodchild.

Chapel Street, looking towards St. Anns Street. Courtesy of James Tuck.

Another view of Chapel Street. Courtesy of James Tuck.

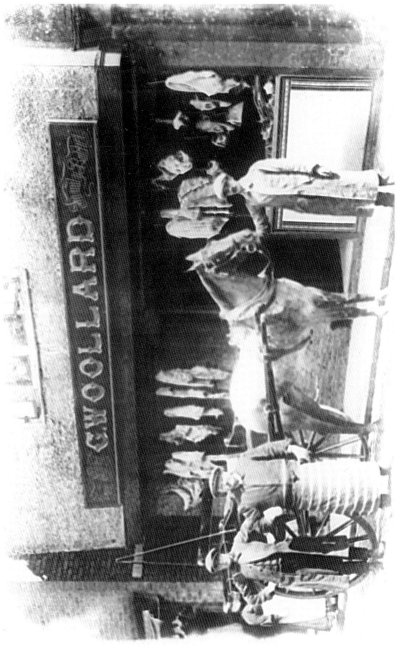

An earlier photograph of Woollards butchers, Chapel Street. Courtesy of Dick Goodchild.

Chapel Street, with view of Black Horse public house. Courtesy of James Tuck.

Lattice House when still the St. Nicholas vergers house. Courtesy of Trues Yard.

ST NICHOLAS STREET

WHITES HOUSE now offices.
ST. NICHOLAS DRILLHALL MINISTRY OF PENSIONS.
DUKE OF CONNAUGHT public house, demolished.
ST. NICHOLAS CHAMBERS, now all car park.
BOWDITCH shopkeeper.
TOWER HILL TRANSPORT CO (now part of TUDOR ROSE).
WALL & SONS ICE CREAM MANUFACTURERS.
ERMINGTON HOUSE (now EMPLOYMENT EXCHANGE).
OXLEY CHAMBER OF TRADE & COMMERCE.
PICKFORDS REMOVAL.

ST. ANNS STREET, LEFT SIDE

THE NAVAL RESERVE public house (incorporated into Trues
Yard).
BARRONS printers.
PORTER gents hairdresser, previously known as Barber Seamans.
HUMPHREYS ship chandlers.
As you passed the shop the smell of new rope, also oakum which
was used for caulking seams in wooden boats.

CHAPEL YARD

ST. NICHOLAS CHAPEL.

ST. ANNS STREET RIGHT SIDE

HARRY SOUTHGATE grocer, post office & ship chandler.
Harry officiated at the Sunday service at the Methodist Chapel
in Pilot St.
ST. ANNS HOUSE.
ST. NICHOLAS MISSION HALL, in what was known as Ship Lane.
Where childrens bible & needlework classes were held, also used
for wedding receptions.
ST. NICHOLAS VICARAGE (now the TUDOR ROSE).

Tudor Rose before becoming a restaurant. Courtesy of Eastern Daily Press.

St. Nicholas Chapel. Courtesy of Lynn News.

Humphreys Ship Chandlers. Courtesy of Trues Yard.

Naval Reserve, now incorporated into Trues Yard. Courtesy of Trues Yard.

Harry Southgate with brother George outside Harry's shop. Courtesy of Trues Yard.

View of Dock Hotel from St. Anns Street. Courtesy of Lynn News.

NORTH STREET

This street holds many memories for us older linnets.
Another of my routes into town if going to the Tuesday Market
or High Street, passing Benefers shop where Mr Benefer would
often be seen standing outside his doorway. I can only remember
once going into North place (the Bone Yard as it was known),
when very young with my Mother to visit an Aunt.

John Southgate had a Shop on the opposite side of the street,
where I would sometimes buy vegetables.

Some of my Husbands friends lived in Begleys Yard and Whitening
Yard. By 1958 many had moved out, with the exception of a few
people. The clearance of North End had begun, houses, shops and
yards standing empty. With the movement of the Northenders,
families who belonged to the fishing quarter of Lynn had only
their memories left of a proud community.

In 1965 after the birth of my daughter, the first time I ventured out
with the pram I had to walk in the middle of the road, the
demolition almost complete, John Kennedy Road was under
construction. Opening In 1966, this was the finish of the North End
that I knew.

Trues Yard Fishing Museum. Courtesy of Trues Yard.

NORTH STREET
LEFT SIDE

From the corner terraced houses and yards. Harry Willis ran a
shop known as Carries.
The Dock Tavern long since closed as a public house.
Trues Yard, houses until John Southgate's shop.
Now the site of Trues Yard Fishing Museum.

NORTH STREET
RIGHT SIDE

On the corner of North Street & Pilot Street Benefers Shop.
Bennels shoe shop, where Mr Bennel could be seen in the window
busily mending boots and shoes with an unrivalled dexterity.
A house where my Husbands father was born.
White Frying Pan fish & chip shop.
Whitening Yard had several houses, one in which my Grandfather
was born.
Further houses.
Begleys Yard.
Further houses.
F. Castleton & Son fish merchant.
North Place. Known as the Bone Yard.
R. Gladding newsagent, formally Biggs.
Three houses.
Dock Hotel public house, publican W. Kemp.
All demolished, site now occupied by Johnsons Garage, Page &
Bird Tyres, Sue Mebbrey Fabrics and Car Wash.

Trues Yard Fishing Museum. Courtesy of Trues Yard.

John Southgate Shop before becoming Trues Yard. Courtesy of Trues Yard.

North Place, North Street. Courtesy of Trues Yard.

PILOT STREET

I lived in Cresswell St until I was married, my only way into Town was via Pilot Street or North Street, depending where in the town I wanted to go. If on my way to work it would be Pilot Street, cycling over the cobbled roadway, passing houses, shops and yards, that I had known since my early childhood. The smell of fish & chips as I passed Rosies, or stopping at Booth's for sweets. I often wondered as I looked at the old St. Nicholas School, later the Shoe Factory, how many children had walked over the same cobbled road to school. I know my Mother and Father both attended there.

Later when I was married I often stopped at Vic Kirby's wet fish shop for smoked haddock, cod roe and winkles which we would sometimes have as a Sunday tea treat.

The Methodist Chapel I never ventured into, to me it seemed from the outside a sombre place. I do remember going to the Pilot Cinema as a child to see Snow White, and during the war to the Saturday morning picture show, the serial Flash Gordon always keeping us children in suspense until the next week. I also visited the Cinema as an adult. Since closing as a cinema the Pilot has been a D.I.Y STORE at the front, a SNOOKER HALL at the back where the seating used to be. Now it is a Nightclub.

PILOT STREET LEFT SIDE

THE TILDEN SMITH public house (now THE RETREAT).
DISUSED RAILWAY LINE.
That once took rail traffic onto the docks this flourished in the fifties, now goods are transported by road.
FISHERMENS RETURN public house,
publican Mrs C. BARNARD locally known as Aunt Charlotte's.

PILOT CINEMA (now ZOOTS NIGHTCLUB).
The cinema showed up to the minute films, and was also occasionally used for live entertainment.

METHODIST CHAPEL demolished with the building of John Kennedy Road.

Private House.

FISHERMANS ARMS public house, publican A. Misson.

Three houses.

BOOTHS confectioners.

R. SMITH fish & chip shop, known as Rosie's.

Two houses.

KIRBY wet fish & shellfish merchant.

Two more houses.

VAN PELTS pork butchers, later a second hand shop.

Many yards were also in Pilot Street, HALF MOON YARD, BROOKES YARD, GRAMPUS YARD, BIRDS YARD. Only a few of the original houses remain

PILOT STREET RIGHT SIDE

Where the railway crossing is, a wooden bridge once spanned the line. The only way to cross, unless one wanted to wait for a considerable time as the train slowly rumbled past.

Walking over the bridge with a pram was no easy task, if caught on the bridge as the engine went under, you would be engulfed in the billowing smoke that swept upwards.

The house next to the bridge Mrs Yaxley lived in, she sold shellfish and samphire when in season. On the corner was Benefers shop.

NORTH STREET

Continuing Pilot Street, more houses, and John Bull's bakery. ST. NICHOLAS SCHOOL FOR BOYS & GIRLS. Where many of the North End children attended. The school closed prior to the Second World War, later as J.S. SOUTHALL'S shoe factory, known as the Snake pit.

All this side of Pilot Street demolished, new housing has taken its Place.

The Exorcists house tucked neatly in the corner by the small
entrance gate that leads into St. Nicholas Chapel survived the
Demolition.
Terraced houses to Austin Street demolished, now Fred Juniper
House on the Site.

Benefers Shop. Courtesy of Trues Yard.

Pilot Street, before demolition. Courtesy of Trues Yard.

Methodist Chapel, Pilot Street. Courtesy of Trues Yard.

Half Moon Yard, Pilot Street. Courtesy of Trues Yard.

St. Nicholas School. (Later Shoe Factory, before demolition). Courtesy of Trues Yard.

St. Nicholas School for Boys & Girls, Pilot Street. Courtesy of J. Walker.

AUSTIN STREET FROM CHAPEL STREET

Austin Street like many others in Lynn was demolished, Six Houses, Blyth's House, another house, Co-Op Dairy and an archway, part of the Austin Friars are all that remain.

Eleven houses (site is now part of car park).
ALBERT ST. LEFT SIDE FROM AUSTIN ST. JOHNSONS SQUARE AND EAST ST. All demolished (now also car park).
Garland Yard, Twelve Houses and Swarby car hire, now car park.
Two Houses.
AUSTIN PLACE.
Seven houses.
HOPE YARD.   Now all part of JOHN KENNEDY ROAD.
Two houses.
RAILWAY PASSAGE.
Two houses.
KING'S LYNN CO-OPERATIVE SOCIETY WAREHOUSE. (now site of LIDL store).

LEFT SIDE

Two houses (now FRED JUNIPER HOUSE).
BLYTH coal merchant (now a private house).
House.
H. SHAW nurseryman.
POST OFFICE ENGINEERING, ORIGINALLY M&GN RAILWAY OFFICE.
Shaw & Post Office engineering (now site of REGIS HOUSE & PRIORY HOUSE).
ALLOTMENTS (now Site of AUSTIN FIELDS INDUSTRIAL ESTATE).

Austin Street, looking towards Littleport Street. Courtesy of Lynn News.

Albert Street, looking towards Norfolk Street. Courtesy of James Tuck.

119

LATER DEMOLITION THAT TOOK PLACE
IN KING'S LYNN

SOUTH CLOUGH LANE, RUSSELL PLACE, REGENTS STREET,
MELBOURNE STREET, BENTINCK STREET,
WHINCOP STREET, BLACKFRIARS STREET
(PARTIALLY TO THE CLOUGH FLEET TAVERN).
ALL OF ST JAMES ROAD, TO THE POLICE STATION.
ALL NOW SITE OF ST JAMES SWIMMING POOL AND CAR PARK.

LOWER CANADA

PAXTON TERRACE, DILKE STREET, WYATT STREET,
OLD TOWN WALL public house the exception, now a private
house.
READ STREET, COAL STREET, COBURG STREET,
PART OF BLACKFRIARS ROAD

HIGHGATE

STAG ROW, LONG ROW, EXHIBITION TERRACE, FRONT ROW,
GARDEN ROW, DOUBLE ROW, all rebuilt.

WINDSOR ROAD

PLEASANT ROW, WINDSOR TERRACE, GARDEN ROW,
COCKLESHELL WALK, VICTORIA STREET,
KEPPLE STREET, DOURO STREET, WELLINGTON STREET.

MILLFLEET & FRIARS AREA

MORGANS BREWERY, HILLINGTON SQUARE,
CORONATION SQUARE, CROOKED LANE, UNION STREET,
NORTH SIDE OF ALL SAINTS STREET, EAST SIDE OF
BRIDGE STREET, PROVIDENCE STREET, NOW THE SITE
OF THE NEW HILLINGTON SQUARE.
The only places exempt from demolition were the ANCIENT
JEWISH CEMETERY, LINCOLN TAVERN and ST. MARGARETS
SCHOOL (now a social club).
The Millfleet was the bus station up to the demolition.

View of South Clough Lane. Courtesy of James Tuck.

Blackfriars Street, looking towards Baxters Plain, Clough Fleet Tavern on left. Courtesy of James Tuck.

Blackfriars Street, looking towards St. Johns Church. Courtesy of James Tuck.

St. James Road, view from Park. All dwellings demolished, now site of swimming pool and car park. Courtesy of James Tuck.

Another view of St. James Road. Courtesy of James Tuck.

Part of Highgate, before demolition. Courtesy of J. Walker.

View of the Millfleet when it was the bus station. Courtesy of James Tuck.

127

An earlier view of the Millfleet when still a waterway.
Courtesy of J. Walker.

Aerial view of waterfront Courtesy of Dick Goodchild.

Aerial view of town. Courtesy of College of West Anglia. © Lynn News

EPILOGUE

To conclude, I hope you have had as much pleasure browsing through this book, and reminiscing about the town as it was, as I had compiling it.

Much of the old town I knew was removed during the late Sixties in the name of progress, now once again certain areas are to be revamped in the near future, with the present century taking us further forward.

King's Lynn of the nineteen Fifties and Sixties has been consigned to history, therefore with the writing of this book and the era covered, I hope I have captured the image of Lynn before the demolition.

Perhaps in another thirty or forty years, someone will undertake the writing of how King's Lynn looked in 2002.

Author